25 Ways
Avoid th

Elizabeth Hill

Copyright Statement

This publication is the full copyright of Elizabeth Hill.

For information contact:

coachingtoconfidence@gmail.com

ISBN – 13   978 -1539069430
ISBN – 10   1539069435

Also by Elizabeth Hill:

25 Steps to Achieving your *MAJOR* Goals – Dare to Dream

Contents

Introduction
Page 7

Who am I?
Or Rather, Who I am
Page 8

Starting Over:
The Myth of Middle Age
Page 11

Life – Where Are You Now?
Page 15

Have an Attitude of Gratitude
Page 19

I'm not Good Enough!
Page 24

The World Looks Kind of
Different Now!
Page 27

To Fear Failure is to Fear Life
Page 30

Toxic Relationships:
Is yours one of them?
Page 33

Letting Go
Page 36

A Little Faith is all it Takes
Page 40

7 Years and 4 Months
Page 44

Don't Look Like This
in the Real World
Page 47

Unleash your Inner Artist!
Page 51

Reasons to be Grateful
for a Recession
Page 54

Work Happier, not Harder
Page 57

Who do you CHOOSE to be?
Page 59

Top 10 Tips for Creating
Your Ideal Life
Page 64

Time to Start Asking the Questions
that will Change Your Life
Page 67

Use Time Wisely –
Don't Try to "Manage" it
Page 69

Chickens and the Art of Mindfulness –
Page 73

Use Your Mind
Page 78

Top 10 Tips for Tackling that Project
Page 81

A Sports Car, a Toyboy and the Kids!
Page 86

Happy Valentine's Day
Page 90

Build Your Own Power Base
Page 94

A Celebration of Thanks
Page 100

This is NOT The End
Page 103

Introduction

I believe that there is a greatness within each and every one of us. I also believe that it is in what is known as 'middle age' and beyond, that we have the intelligence, the resources and the maturity to discover this greatness – and to act upon it.

You may not discover the next Einstein or Picasso inside of you. But no matter, the world only needs a few of these in every generation.

What the world needs now are people who are willing to show up as their most loving, glorious self ... and that includes you.

Elizabeth Hill
August 2016

Who am I? Or Rather, Who I am

My name is Elizabeth Hill.

I am ordinary in many respects. I am a middle class, 40 something, a single mother of 4 children.

I am, however, extraordinary in one respect:

I love the life that I am living.

I have spent the last 15 years of my life on a quest to find real happiness and create my ideal life. Of course I have my off days when things don't go well, but they are part of life. The thing about my life is that it is ordinary. The fact that I am happy with my life does not depend upon a well-stocked bank account or the perfect relationship and that is good news for those of you who are looking to create your own ideal lives.

This project has fascinated me so much that I began to research why some people seemed happy in life and others didn't. My research has led me to examine the lives of women from the ages of 35(ish) and up and to see if any common patterns seemed to emerge in the lives of those women who expressed dissatisfaction with life. This dissatisfaction ranged from a mild feeling of life passing them by; to the feeling that they were no longer living a life that matched their values; to a much more serious form in which women felt their usefulness in life was severely diminished.

This book is about the challenges that many women face in negotiating those years in which perhaps your relationships with others have changed (divorce, children no longer need you in that intense, all consuming way that they did when they were young), life has lost the excitement of youth and the feeling that everything is possible, or simply that you are living a life which is not the one that you imagined.

Having survived the ending of a marriage, the loss I felt as my role of carer to my children slowly slipped away and I began to make way for the next generation to take centre stage, in the realisation that life had not turned out the way that I had planned, or hoped, I began to realise that the lessons that life was teaching me could be reframed and used for setting the stage for the rest of my life.

I now believe that life in 'middle age' can be the most truly satisfying of our existence. Yes, we may have to reframe our perspectives to achieve this belief but once we do, there is no limit to the life we can live, the things we can achieve and the benefits we can bring to the world.

These chapters are all standalone pieces so please feel free to read them in any order. In fact, I encourage you to read them in any order that suits you.

Starting Over: The Myth of Middle Age

I realised recently that I have acquired a superpower. It comes in very handy at times and at other times it is rather annoying. On balance I like having this superpower.

"What is it?" you ask.

It is the power of invisibility! Useful for walking unnoticed past groups of drunken lads out for the night. Not so useful, however, if I am trying to attract the attention of a shop assistant!

How did I acquire this superpower?

Well, I entered middle age. This appears to be the time when we tend to slip out of public consciousness. We no longer hold attention because of our youth and our looks but we are yet to register on the 'concern for the elderly' lists. In short, we tend to slip through the net of society's consciousness. To see those in mid life as irrelevant, however, is a mistake.

It has been said that we spend the first 40 years of our life gathering parts of our soul together and then the next 40 years putting them to good use.

So what experiences, skills, qualities and preferences have you gathered in life so far?

And now, most importantly, how are you going to put them to good use?

How are you going to express the best possible you and how would you like to contribute to the overall happiness in the world?

For that is what it is time to do. No longer being concerned with trying to fit into a life you 'should' be living, you now have the wisdom and experience to know what kind of conditions you need to thrive. Perhaps you have finished raising a family, or come to the end of a career which once thrilled you. Now you can look up from your own environment and begin to wonder what sort of a world you would like to pass down to future generations. If it is different from the one you see in front of you, then any changes you wish for begin with you – with your knowledge and experiences.

What would you like to change and why?

How can you teach your children, your community, your workplace, how much life is worth?

How do all the elements you have experienced help to colour your vision of the world?

This task is not to be left to a few select politicians. We have seen many times that the vision others have for this world is not our vision of how the world could be. Perhaps you would like the world to contain more equality, for rich and poor, for men and women. Perhaps you have environmental concerns or you would like to teach people how to live in a less consumerist society. Perhaps you want to be an example of an individual who leads a balanced life. In mid life we have the skills and the knowledge to do this. We are able to express ourselves authentically and to show younger generations what is possible. We are old enough to protest about the problems of the world and young enough to do something about it.

What is the point of going through the experiences we have had in life if not to learn from them and then to put that knowledge to good use in creating a better world?

The people who do this are the ones that have the greatest impact on humanity, not the politicians tinkering with different policies.

So use your powers of invisibility wisely! But equally find the power of authenticity within you, too and be prepared to unleash it on the world. We need you more than ever before!

Life – Where Are You Now?

A song came on the radio the other day – 'Jack and Diane', by John Cougar. Growing up in the 80's the song played a big part in my teenage years. I admit it, I had a massive crush on the singer but I also loved that song about two American kids growing up and the dreams they had. I could still remember the words as I sang along to it when it came on the air last week (typical, I can remember the words of an 80's pop song but not to put money on my son's dinner money account!). But this time as I sang along I was struck by the phrase: *'Oh yeh, life goes on, long after the thrill of living is gone.'*

Suddenly that truth hit me, how true that as we grow up our dreams seem to be replaced by what we would call the realities of life, that life was no longer new and exciting. Instead we cling to security at any cost, more anxious to preserve the status quo than to seek out new challenges. We become more conservative, more fearful and more cynical as we move into new phases of life.

I have been guilty of this recently myself. As the youngest of my four children has taken his first steps towards independence I know that my role as a full time mother is coming to an end and just as someone who has just been made redundant from a job they loved, I too have to grieve what is ending and to start looking for a new challenge, to find once more the thrill of living albeit in a different form to the one I once had.

This is not an easy thing to achieve. We look back at the past and wish we could live that life for just a little longer. We are scared to let go of who we once were and step into who we are becoming. No longer do we have the dreams that teenagers are capable of conjuring up with their unlimited optimism that the future will be brighter. We have seen too many disappointments and reality checks for us to take notice of the power of our imagination.

But whilst teenagers may have the optimism, it is those in later life who have the skills, experience and the knowledge of themselves and what makes them happy who are in a position to look at all the options which are available to them (and nowadays the choice is vast) and to craft a life which suits them. It takes time and effort to stop and think how you would like your life to be but therein lies the thrill of life by putting the steps in place to live a life of your own choosing.

When you gaze around you at the world that you live in, which elements bring you joy, pain, boredom?

What about me?

I have spent several months exploring my options – taking some elements on board and discarding others. I look around at the world I live in and there are some elements of the world that I feel passionately about changing. For example I believe that my work / life balance is important and that a portfolio of jobs is an option which has been underdeveloped within society. I believe that in a rush to obtain more and more we are actually gaining less and less and these are things that I hope to address. And as the ancient Chinese proverb says these changes all begin with me.

The thrill of life has reappeared and I shall carry on chasing it for a little while at least! I would love to hear what ignites the thrill of life for you and together we can make this a world in which happiness is the preserve of many and not just a lucky few.

Have an Attitude of Gratitude

Gratitude - Part 1

The first step to living a wonderful life is to recognise which parts of your life are already wonderful. Look at your family, your friends, your home, and your health. Take the time to appreciate what you already have in your life and look at it with a sense of gratitude.

Gratitude - Part 2

When you have made a list (mental or otherwise) of all the things and people that make your life wonderful, notice the pleasure they bring you on a daily basis.

What would you miss if they weren't around any more?

Cultivate an awareness of the little things that make you happy, things that are easily overlooked because we take them for granted. Remember the excitement you first felt when you went out with your partner, got that job or how you felt when you got your new car.

Do you still feel the same excitement and pleasure when you get into your car now?

If not, take time to re-kindle those feelings by noting how good it makes you feel to drive it to places, kiss your partner or hold your daughter's hand. These are the things that make our lives wonderful and yet these feelings often pass unnoticed because we are too busy chasing that perfect life.

Gratitude - Part 3
Acknowledge those parts of your life you do not enjoy or cause you stress and be thankful for them....yes, really! Because...

a. You may have learnt a valuable lesson from them or...

b. You have been offered the opportunity to try something out that you thought you wanted. Now you realise it doesn't really fit with who you are.

Be grateful for the experience and what you have gained from it and move on to the next experience. This is not always easy to do, even if you know that a certain situation is not a good match for you.

So what can we do to get back on track to that wonderful life?

Start by acknowledging to yourself that you are not happy with your current situation and why. Once you are looking honestly at the situation you find yourself in, begin to analyse what about that situation you can be grateful for.

Has it taught you something valuable about: yourself, other people?

Has it given you the opportunity to try something out that you thought you wanted, but then having done it, realised it wasn't for you?

Are there just certain aspects about the situation you don't like and can these be changed or re-arranged?

I once heard a famous comedian being interviewed on the radio. During the interview he mentioned that long before he made his living from comedy, he had worked in a variety of jobs to support himself. But he refused to work on a Monday, so at each job interview he told the prospective boss that he didn't work on a Monday... he was surprised how many people hired him despite his criteria. So don't dismiss a less than ideal situation out of hand without looking at the alternatives that may be available to you.

Gratitude – Part 4

You may have gathered by now that I believe that gratitude forms the foundations for living a wonderful life. We all know people who have so much in their lives (things that many would be envious of) and yet spend all their time moaning about all that is wrong in their life, or the people who are always chasing the next best thing without stopping to appreciate what they have.

So go on, give gratitude a go. It's free to try and may become addictive!

I'm not Good Enough!

Recently I saw the film, 'The King's Speech', which tells the story of how King George VI battled to overcome his stammer. It may not have been a big issue had his brother not abdicated the throne, but he did, and the rest is history.

King George was a hero in every sense of the word. Ill equipped in his opinion to succeed his regal father and popular brother, he nevertheless had the courage to accept the challenge of becoming the country's monarch in difficult times, despite his lack of self-belief. It is not the purpose of this chapter to discuss which came first, the lack of self-belief or the stammer, but certainly it was an obvious hurdle that he had to overcome if he was to gain the confidence to rule.

But the point of this chapter is to ask whether it is easier to address outward issues such as stammering, which can often, when improved, lead to an increased confidence in oneself, than it is to address that small voice inside of someone that whispers, *'You're not good enough'* whenever you decide to step out of your comfort zone. For when there is no outward indication of this voice, it is very easy to try to ignore it and hope it will just go away. It is often easier for many of us to ask for help with something obvious, than it is to ask for help with the, *'I'm not good enough,'* voice which is also part of your make up.

But, make no mistake; this voice can seriously sabotage your self-belief. It can begin as a whisper and can often be hidden at first behind an apparent air of self-confidence. It is often this little voice that stops us doing the things that we would really love to do and we exert much energy in trying to silence this voice – hiding it from friends, family and colleagues.

The great thing about the, *'I'm not good enough,'* voice that I have discovered, however, is that once it is acknowledged, it is very often found to have no substance whatsoever. The only thing that was sustaining it was the energy spent trying to ignore it. Once you bring it out into the open and hold it up to examination, you can see almost immediately that it is far less scary than it ever felt before and in fact I have to say that sometimes I have even laughed at the ridiculous things that it whispers!

So if you have an, *'I'm not good enough,'* voice lurking somewhere within – let it out – poke around a bit to see what substance lies within it, (*'Good enough for what, exactly?'*) and then just let it go and replace it with a voice that says, *'I'm absolutely fabulous!'*

The World Looks Kind of Different Now!

Well, it has been a while since I finished work and decided to pursue other things. It was a leap of faith – I did not know where my journey would take me – only that it was time to move on. It has been a time of many changes, some visible to the outside world and some visible only to me. Last night however, I caught myself beating myself up for all the things that I hadn't, *'ticked off my list'*, during this time; for instance, I am not yet a multi-millionaire and neither has the vegetable garden materialised.

So I sat down and listed all the things that I am proud of achieving in this past year and as I wrote, the list got longer and longer. It ranged from the trivial – I can now make brilliant cupcakes – to the momentous – I now have my own business and my own radio show. I acquired two rescue dogs who are now very much part of the family. I learnt that I am a 'third culture kid' and how to stop my ego pushing in when my intuition is trying to tell me something.

In short, when I started to write my list I was amazed at how much my life had changed in the space of a year. No longer do I want to beat myself up for not having achieved certain goals (ok maybe the multi-millionaire aim was more of a pipe-dream!), I am proud of myself for extending my comfort zone just a little bit further. In fact I feel like a caterpillar that knew it was time to change but didn't know what was waiting for him the other side of the cocoon. The view looks very different from up here – there will be other challenges from now on and my boundaries will be pushed a little more. I don't know what lies ahead but I do know that I will meet life's challenges to the best of my ability.

Sometimes we all need to remind ourselves that whereas once we were like a caterpillar, time has moved us on and without noticing, we have turned into a butterfly – that life has thrown us challenges and we rose to the occasion. Sometimes it takes others to remind us of how far we have come but, ultimately, it is you who must step up to the stage and show the world who you have become.

To Fear Failure is to Fear Life

J.K. Rowling and I share something very significant in common. No, sadly, I am not a world-class author! However, perhaps what we share is of more significance than a series of books and a number of blockbusting films. Well, maybe not - but she gave a Commencement Speech in 2008 at the award of her Honorary Degree at Harvard University - in which she stated she had been as close to rock bottom as it was possible to have been, without being homeless.

She had failed in her marriage; her career and personal life were crumbling around her. I too have been to that place, and scary as it was at the time (I had 4 young children relying solely on me) I look back, as does J K Rowling and in her words, '*I was set free because my greatest fear had been realised*'. Once you get to Rock Bottom, there is nowhere to go but up. We spend so much time and energy struggling to keep from hitting rock bottom, that we are not looking towards the mountains and planning how to get to the top.

I cannot pretend that I found enjoyable, the period of time in which I had no money, no possessions and no one to turn to. Like many others who have reached *that place* though, I realised that in stripping away everything, the only thing I had to rely on was myself and the desire to give my children a good life. Looking back now, I feel grateful for all the lessons that time taught me.

The biggest lesson of all that it taught me was not to fear failure. That failure is part of living your biggest life.

How else do you expand your comfort zone, if not to stretch out your abilities just a little more?

Too little and you never move towards your dreams; too much and you may experience needless failure; but get that level of failure right and your life can be transformed in a way that you could never have imagined.

As J. K. Rowling summed it up in what is perhaps, one of the greatest lines she has written so far: '*It is impossible to live without failing at something, unless you live so cautiously that you might as well not have lived at all – in which case, you fail by default.*'

Don't live your life by default. Go on give yourself permission not to be perfect!

Toxic Relationships: Is yours one of them?

Do any of your relationships with your partner, family and friends or work colleagues, leave you feeling drained?

If so, you may be the victim of an energy vampire. Energy vampires are people who are attracted to you because of your high energy and feed off it, as they are unable to access their own.

To give you an example of this type of relationship, a close friend of mine recently finished with her boyfriend. Whilst in this relationship, once a bubbly, positive person, she changed into a person who lacked energy, often had headaches and stomach aches and generally became very negative in her outlook on life. She had been unhappy for a long time but lacked the energy to break off the relationship. Eventually she did finish it and immediately her energy levels began to rise dramatically. Her frequent headaches disappeared; as did the asthma which she had developed over the period she had been seeing him (he was also an asthmatic).

As her energy levels began to rise again and her health improved, so her mood began to lighten and her naturally positive outlook became apparent once more. She also had the energy to clear out the clutter that had accumulated during this time.

So examine your own energy levels. If they are usually high and you are full of life until you are with a certain person and you feel your energy draining away -it is literally taken by the other person – beware. Cast a critical eye over your significant relationships.

Do you walk away from time spent with a person, uplifted or depressed?

Once we become aware of how others make us feel, we are able to make choices as to whether we want to continue in this relationship or not. Energy vampires often latch on to people who are naturally very giving and even if you break up with them, they will try very hard to persuade you to go back to them – using their available energy to exert an influence on you. But be warned – they cannot sustain that level of energy for long and will start living off your energy again before too long.

Or do you have permanently low energy levels and consistently try to take it from others?

If this is happening, you need to access your own energy. It IS within you, albeit you may have to search some dusty corner to find it. Look inwards, not outwards to find what excites and inspires you. Once you can identify one thing others will follow. Be selfish with your energy. Get to know how much to give out at any one time and how to replenish it when you are running on empty. And never give away your own energy for somebody else to use.

Letting Go

After 21 years of living with me, my daughter is moving out – to a new home. What is a time of great excitement is also a time of great sadness for me. I have to accept the fact that she is no longer my little girl and we must form a new relationship, as adults, together. The lessons I have taught her about life will be taken with her and either put into practice or discarded as she sees fit. My role as her mother will not cease, but it will change. It is as it should be. I am proud that I have raised a confident, independent woman; but part of me would like to go back – just for one day – to a time in which her entire world revolved around me. I am left wondering whether I appreciated every single moment with her as fully as possible.

But change is inevitable. Many people use up enormous amounts of energy trying to resist change and letting go is perhaps the biggest hurdle we face in this process. For some of us letting go of material objects is very easy, but letting go of people is much harder. For others, it is difficult to let go of the material – houses, jobs or possessions. Especially in this economic climate, we spend much of our time trying to hang on to something; not because it serves our best interests but because it feels safe and secure – we are in our comfort zone.

However, one of the purposes of all of our lives *is* to expand our comfort zones as far as they will go! If we did not, the human race would not survive. It is change, which helps us to do this. Once we have mastered one challenge we are shown another. Babies are given an enormous number of different challenges to deal with in a very short space of time – to learn to smile, then walk and talk. They do these things willingly, as they have not yet learnt to resist change. For them change is fun and exciting, and so it should be for us as adults.

Change becomes easier to bear when we realise that letting go of things/ people / situations does not make us less of a person unless we allow it to. Change is designed to make us more of a person – it allows new situations into our lives and hence allows us to grow.

My role as a mother will change as I am no longer required to cook, wash and provide a home for my daughter; but as this role diminishes, so new opportunities come in and I will develop as a person in other areas of my life.

Accepting that change is inevitable can bring us an appreciation of what is in our lives at this moment. Knowing for certain that one day we will not be in our current job (whether due to redundancy or retirement) can help us appreciate all that we love about it at this moment. How easy it is to take a loved one for granted, but one day they will no longer be here and knowing this allows us to feel appreciative of what we share right now.

So while I allow myself to feel sadness at my daughter's departure, I also allow myself to feel the tingle of anticipation as I await the new opportunities that life has to offer me. Once more I am on a journey to expand my comfort zone!

A Little Faith is all it Takes

Whenever people ask me what I do for a living and I tell them that I help people to create their ideal life, I often see their eyebrows rise slightly. And if I could read people's thoughts, I am pretty sure they would be, '*Yeh right of course we can all have our ideal life with Brad Pitt hanging off our arm and the Ferrari in the garage*'. But (and this is a crucial 'but'), most people's image of their ideal life is not, when they stop and think about it, like that at all (the obvious exception to this image is his partner's, hopefully!).

It is my belief that our ultimate purpose on earth is for us to grow into the best person that we can be and in order to do this we need the right kind of environment for us. So when I am coaching people they do not come out of the process owning a 12 bedroomed mansion and dating a tall, dark handsome film star (if they did I would have far more clients than I could ever handle!). But they come out with something far more valuable. They come out having discovered the type of life which will bring them joy and purpose. They may want to include certain material things within this lifestyle but it is not usually the primary aim. Most of us can point to people that we know who apparently live what many would class an ideal life (the glamorous career, the loving spouse, the big house and wonderful kids) and still not be happy. These unhappy people are simply not in an environment in which they can live their ideal life.

Achieving this life does not of course mean that you will live happily ever after. We cannot eliminate stress from our lives completely, whether you are leading your ideal life or not, there will always be that leaking tap or argument with a friend. However within your ideal environment, these problems are just part of everyday life. Hopefully you are living a life in which you have a clear idea of what you want – what makes you happy and a vision of how to get it. I do not have everything that I want in life, but I am working my way towards certain goals and I am enjoying the journey.

So some questions to ask yourself when creating your ideal life:

Where am I happiest?

Do you like the excitement of a busy office? Do you prefer being at home? In the town or the country?

With whom am I happiest?

Family? Friends? On your own? In a crowd?

What activities make me happiest?

Work? Hobbies? Family?

What pace do you like life to take?

Hectic? High Pressured? Slow?

These are just some of the questions you can use as the basis for creating your ideal life and, I believe, we underestimate our own power and greatness if we do not acknowledge that creating our ideal life is within the grasp of each and every one of us.

7 Years and 4 Months

7 years and 4 months – that is the time it took me to renovate my house. It was at Christmas time that I renovated the last 2 remaining rooms in my house.

Why am I telling you this?

It is because the work I have done on my house is a reflection of the work I have done on myself over that same period of time.

I moved into my house following my divorce but unlike in me, most of the cracks in the building did not show up immediately. It took a few weeks for the neglect of the house to become apparent. Collapsing ceilings, dry rot, rotten joists and insect infestation all showed up over the years. The house has been extended, re-plastered, had most of the ceilings replaced along with a new kitchen and bathroom. In other words, it is only really the foundations, which have been left untouched. I wasn't expecting to do any of this work when I moved in (I had never done any DIY before in my life and I certainly did not welcome the intrusion!).

But I am extremely proud of myself as I look around at what I have achieved here. I am proud of the fact that I rose to challenges that I would never have believed myself capable of and I am proud of the fact that I was able to raise the money to pay for the specialist work to be done. Somewhere along the way I realised that for the house to become structurally sound, it would mean creating more mess and confusion before it looked any better.

I also realised that the same thing was happening to me, too. I would begin to build up a certain level of confidence and then something would happen to make me doubt my abilities to make my way in the world. Like the renovations of my house, in order to get to the next level, I would need to go through a period of mess and confusion before coming out the other side with stronger foundations having been put in place.

I believe that our purpose in life is to grow into the best person we can be. For me, I came to appreciate that in creating a home out of what has seemed to be a building site for the best part of seven years, has been instrumental in giving me the foundations needed to build the next part of my life. Now I have other challenges to face and I realise that there will be times when I am again faced with mess and confusion but what awaits on the other side is, I hope, worth it.

I wish you many great challenges for the coming year and I hope when you come through them; the view on the other side is wonderful!

Don't Look Like This in the Real World

'Don't Look Like This In The Real World', so said the advert for Fake Bake Tan, a poster that used to hang on the wall where I worked. The advert shows a picture of 2 women, one standing in a provocative pose, in the hope that she will be noticed and the other looking less visible in trying to attract attention, but more self-assured.

Miley Cyrus once made headline news with her provocative poses in her music videos. This has raised a few questions in my mind.

First - *What drives the need in us to want attention from other people; especially from those we don't know?*

Second - *Are the qualities that we possess not enough to hold people's interest?*

Third - *Do we always have to be revealing more and more of ourselves, both physically and mentally to hold the interest of another?*

We all need to be noticed, to be loved. Unsurprisingly evolution must have taught us that if the tribe does not notice us, we may be left behind, overlooked when it comes to getting food etc.

But putting aside our biological make-up – why do we feel the need to gain attention from others, people whom we don't even know?

Could it be that we need validation that we are ok / that we are worthwhile?

What happens if that validation is taken away from us?

Nowadays it is not just celebrities who live out their lives in public – so do we, on Facebook, Twitter and other social media (even if we are only having a coffee somewhere!). We are so used to seeking approval from others however that when it is taken away, we cannot cope.

It happened to me when I was married. For years I had done all I could to seek approval from others in bringing up kids, being a wife and living life as others saw fit. When my marriage crumbled and people disapproved of me the consequences were devastating. I had needed their approval to prop up the sham that had become my life. Without that approval, I was left contemplating just how fake I had become; how far removed I was from my own values and from what truly made me happy. I am lucky this happened to me when I was relatively young. For many the realisation that they have been living a lie solely for the approval of other people only strikes them on their deathbed – too late to try to turn their life around.

As for me, well, ironically losing many of my family and friends was perhaps the best thing that could happen to me. In hindsight at least! I was left with a solid core of friends who loved me no matter what. I no longer had to live a life to please others and was free to be who I truly was. And to be honest, I have to say I like myself a whole lot more than when everybody liked me. It takes time to build up your own powerbase and to know that you are ok just the way you are.

No, in fact you are more than ok. You are just what the world needs!

Unleash your Inner Artist!

Do you shudder when you look back at your school days and your attempts in art, needlework or music?

Or do you look back with fond memories of a time spent happily messing about with lumps of clay?

Everybody has a creative side to them, but as we get older we seldom take the time to flex our creativity 'muscles', often believing that creativity is a luxury that we have no time to indulge in, that it has no place in our busy lives – I disagree. Worse still, even if we do have a secret longing to be more creative we worry that the artist within us has been in hibernation for too long to ever see the light of day again!

So I urge you to start looking for that inner artist once more. Everybody is creative; it is a vital part of our self – development. We were all put on earth to create – to add value to the world. Your creativity may not appear in the usual activities such as drawing, painting or playing the flute; but start looking for the areas in which your creativity does show up.

Does it appear in your cooking as you adapt or invent new recipes to create a culinary masterpiece?

Is it in the way that you interact with your children – inventing stories or making a pirate boat out of a cardboard box?

Do you have a talent for putting clothes together to form a fabulous outfit?

Take time to identify where your creative talents lie (ask family and friends if you are really stuck) and start taking steps to unleash that inner artist. You can start with baby steps and be gentle with yourself. Put the withering looks from your 3rd Form teacher firmly out of your mind and take yourself to an art class or a dance workshop. Leave any expectations of creating a masterpiece behind and go and have fun making mistakes – even if you decide painting is not for you, you have made a start in opening up your creativity. Have fun with it – let it spill out into your job, relationships and free time. For me my writing is a creative outlet. I imagine myself as Michelangelo who said of himself as a sculptor, that he just chipped away at the marble and inside was a statue of David. I sit down and write on a variety of topics and out of those topics I begin to make sense of my relationship to the world, my emotions and my creativity.

Reasons to be Grateful for a Recession

1. CHANGE

It is easy to plod along (or even race along at top speed!) in relatively uneventful times perhaps congratulating ourselves on having a great lifestyle and living in stress-free circumstances. But the purpose of our lives isn't to strive to get to this point. The purpose of our lives is to grow into the best possible person that we can be. At no time does this happen faster than in times of change. And that brings us on to:

2. CHALLENGE

Recession brings us challenges to overcome. Difficult circumstances allow us to widen our perspective of the world (for instance we may gain empathy with those who have very little money, when we suddenly lose our job). We begin to question the values our lives are built on and the image we have of ourselves when faced with challenging circumstances. It is when things go wrong that we realise who and what is important to us. Things are not all bad however for times of recession also bring:

3. OPPORTUNITIES

Opportunities to:
Try a new career
Try a new hobby
Work in the community
Start paying off debts
Spend more time with the family
Plan how to spend money on things that *really* matter

4. DOWNSIZE

Within a recession, opportunities arise to take a good look at our lives and our businesses and see how we can improve and adapt them in order to move forward in a new direction. Looking at our budget means we can identify where money is wasted and we can let go of material possessions that we don't really need. I once walked away from almost an entire household of possessions and with the exception of the odd twinge of regret I felt more liberated than at any other time in my life to be free from all that clutter!

5. RECONNECT

There is nothing more important than the fact that we truly connect with ourselves and give ourselves authentically to the world. It is not always easy and sometimes we find that we have been travelling down a path that isn't really one of our own making. With the rest of the world busy trying to make sense of all these changes for themselves, no one will notice if you decide to travel a different path... go on. I dare you!

Work Happier, not Harder

I tend to look inwards over the winter months thinking about who I have been over the past year and who I wish to become over the coming year. I question what I have done and the things I wish to do next. Coming from sunnier countries, I used to hate the way that winter in England made me feel – often I lacked energy and felt tired when dark fell. Then I realised that winter gave me the greatest opportunities for growth. Now I copy nature and to the outside world when it looks like nothing is happening – no leaves are visible, no flowers are blooming, underneath the soil the hard work is happening and all of a sudden in spring, plants and trees burst into life with a renewed determinism to give their best show yet!

As a culture we are not encouraged to take time out, especially in business. We are urged to work longer and longer hours in the pursuit of our careers and a growing income.

The result is that we stop growing and start existing, running around on the hamster wheel of life, endlessly chasing more – of what?

Do we need to validate our existence to others or earn respect from ourselves?

Do we really need that amount of money to live a valuable life or to maintain our current lifestyle?

If you take time to listen to your body it will give you the answer. If you are working too hard or in the wrong profession the warning signals often come in the form of stress, depression or illness.

So I am putting forward the idea that we follow nature's example and we work happier not harder. Meanwhile the rest of us can watch the glorious displays as the people that we care about blossom into the best human being they can be!

Who do you CHOOSE to be?

I have a friend who used to regularly come to see me. Every time we met he would start to tell me all of the problems he had, how his life was not going well etc. At first I thought that he was going through a tough patch (as we all do from time to time), so I would sit down with him and try to help him find solutions to his problems. This was not what he wanted however. He didn't want to find solutions; he wanted to be the star in his own misery show. I was supposed to sit and commiserate with him about his hard luck, not help him to create a better life! This I refused to do once I realised what was going on.

Why?

Because my friend was choosing to be a person who was a victim in life. He said he hated having these problems that were stopping him from living the life he wanted, but when faced with the opportunity to solve them he didn't want to know.

To solve the problems that you perceive yourself to have, you have to start by choosing to be a person who can rise to the challenge. It is the person who begins to see themselves as responsible for where they find themselves in life right now who can start to understand that they have the power to change their situation also. It is when you choose wisely your thoughts about who you are that mountains are climbed, the universe conspires to help you move forward to your best possible self and miracles occur!

What is the story you tell of your life so far?

Many people do not consciously carry around this story but they do it all the same! This story appears in all your conversations, in all your thoughts about the world and in all your actions. This story contains all the beliefs you have about yourself and it is the most important story ever written.

Consider the following people:

Person A carries around a story that has been built up gradually throughout their life. It goes like this:

'My parents didn't have much money when we were growing up so I never had the opportunities to do things that I would have liked to do. It has been a struggle all of my life to survive and as soon as one crisis is over the universe just throws something else at me. Life is so unfair – if only I was richer, more talented, prettier...etc. life would be so much easier. I married a man who I thought would look after me, but he has just left so I am on my own again, another failure! I can't be bothered to try anything new, as I will only fail at it. Success is something which only happens to other people, not to me.'

Person B on the other hand tells a story which goes like this:

'We had very little money whilst I was growing up but it taught me to live within my means and to know that happiness is not dependent upon money. As I grew up I had loads of opportunities to discover the sort of person I wanted to become or didn't want to become! I made mistakes of course, but some of the biggest challenges I faced (for instance when my husband walked out on me) were in hindsight the biggest opportunities for discovering who I really am. The challenges that I have overcome in the past have made me self-reliant and I feel like a conquering hero every time I achieve one of my goals. I am the only person responsible for creating happiness in my life as only I know what makes me happy.'

Of course **Person A** and **Person B** could be the same person. The only difference between the two people is the thoughts they are *choosing* to have about themselves.

So the question is:

'What story are you choosing to tell about yourself?'

Are you choosing to be a victim, blaming others for your misfortunes or expecting them to take care of you; or are you a hero, who despite setbacks and wrong turns, has the courage and willpower to pick yourself up and dust yourself down as you continue along?

The choice is down to you. So Happy Choosing and whichever way your story reads I wish you luck and good fortune along the way!

Top 10 Tips for Creating Your Ideal Life

1. Cultivate an 'attitude of gratitude'

Give thanks for all the good things that you have in your life at this point. It is a great place to start to make your changes from.

2. Spend time thinking about the person you want to become and what is important in your life

Meditation is a great way to quieten your mind and to allow yourself to step back and see the bigger picture.

3. Set your goals

I write them down (a mixture of small and larger goals) for the different areas of my life that are important to me.

4. Create a vision board

Stick pictures that represent your goals onto a board (e.g. if one of your goals is to move house, find pictures of your ideal home and stick them on). Your brain will find ways to create this as a reality.

5. Focus on the activities which will move you closer to your goal

Too many times we have a goal but instead of spending time on taking steps to achieve it, we spend time on the more immediate tasks in front of us.

6. Practise the art of being selfish

Everybody is entitled to time to herself. Take it and use it wisely!

7. Clear out the old to make way for the new

Clutter / Clothes/ Relationships

8. Invest time in those people who are important to you

There is a saying that says we cannot choose our family, but the fact is, we can choose how much time we spend with both our family and our friends. If somebody drains your energy or dismisses your ideals, your goals, spend your time with them wisely. I have a very close family member who I never discuss my plans with because I know that they will only worry about me and try to dissuade me from erring from the *'path of stability'* that they see is the most sensible option for me. Instead, we limit our conversation to family gossip and other news and then we get along fine.

9. Watch your thoughts

Don't let negative thoughts put you off achieving all you are capable of. Often when we try something new, our Ego tries to sabotage our efforts in order to maintain our place in the comfort zone.

10. Find ways to celebrate the small steps you take along the way

Don't wait until a goal has been achieved to celebrate. Maintain momentum and celebrate each step of the way!

Time to Start Asking the Questions that will Change Your Life

'It's time to ask smarter questions,' urge IBM in one of their recent marketing campaign.

They are right – not just in business, but also of and for ourselves, and what better time to do it than in times of change and uncertainty?

Why?

Because by asking questions: of ourselves, of our beliefs and assumptions, of our direction in life, of our plans and desires and the shape that our lives have taken and will take, we expand our awareness of ourselves. We start to question our ideas and our limits. We can begin to see that many of the restrictions placed upon us are self-imposed.

Questions help us to shift our perspective towards life. In order to create a happy and fulfilling life for ourselves, nothing external has to change, but our thoughts do. This is why we have to start by asking ourselves smarter questions as the advert says.

Questions such as *'Why does this always happen to me?'* take away our power to move forward in life and increase our fear.

The smarter question to ask is *'What can I learn from this situation?'* / *'What is life trying to teach me?'*

The physicist, Bohm, wrote:
'In scientific enquiries, a crucial step is to ask the right question. Indeed, each question contains presuppositions, largely implicit. If these presuppositions are wrong or confused, then the question itself is wrong in the sense that to try to answer it, has no meaning'.

IBM understands that businesses grow and develop by asking the right questions and the same is true of people too.

Use Time Wisely – Don't Try to "Manage" it

When is your Golden Hour?

This question is perhaps one of the most important that you can ask yourself. Let me explain. There is a period of time (possibly an hour or two) in the 24-hour clock that is the time that you are at your most creative and productive. It is in this time that you will get your best work done. This is the passion that feeds your soul, the activity that makes you feel great about yourself and your abilities.

For me the passion that feeds my soul is writing. I love writing articles on any number of topics, for business, for pleasure and mostly for sharing my experiences in order to help those people who can learn from my mistakes a lot quicker than I did! I am also writing a novel. This is my secret passion. I may never publish this novel but it is teaching me so much about myself and my beliefs, the characters have now taken on a life of their own and I am learning from them (sounds crazy I know but it is true). However writing my novel is hard to do when in normal waking hours the world demands that I pay attention to it. The phone rings; a member of my family has a question that needs answering right now; life is generally busy... you get the picture.

I have found however from trial and error that the perfect time for me to write is between 5.30am and 7.30am. I may not use all of this time to write, sometimes I stop and do another activity, but I know that between these hours my concentration meets my creativity and I am functioning at my peak. Occasionally I use this time if I have a particularly complex document to read (such as a contract etc.) as I know that my concentration levels are at their highest and I know that my distractions will be minimal.

Your *'Golden Hour'* may not be at 5.30am. You may work at your best at

2 in the afternoon or at 2 in the morning. My partner likes to work late at night when everybody has gone to bed. I am useless past about 8pm, so everybody has their own golden hour in which they do their best work.

I am not, by the way, talking about the work people do for financial gain (although if you work for yourself it can be) but the work that feeds their soul. As I mentioned, my novel may never be read by anybody but me. I know however that if I write in that Golden Hour, I can go about my daily life knowing that I have achieved something that is worthwhile to me.

The work you do in your Golden Hour is something that you do for yourself (whether or not it benefits anybody else) and in many cases, that you may feel takes second place to your daily activities. It may be making cupcakes; gardening (you will just have to ignore strange looks from neighbours if you find that you garden best at 3.30 in the morning!); or write blog posts on new medical research. It is more than a hobby, it is the passion that makes your heart sing and without its presence in your day, life seems a little bit duller.

Chickens and the Art of Mindfulness

I believe very strongly that we come to live on earth with the intention of growing and evolving into the best possible person that we can be. Problems occur when we forget this mission and instead we throw all our energies into maintaining the status quo – protecting our wealth, our careers and our relationships and our egos. Or we stagnate, we get stuck, knowing that we have taken a wrong direction and not knowing how to get back on track. Fear begins to sap our energy and our enthusiasm for life.

Once you begin to realise however, that your purpose in life is to expand as a person *in any way that you see fit*, life becomes a challenge, an adventure and you become the hero in your own story, You begin to notice the opportunities – the lessons – which life provides for you to help you grow.

One such lesson came to me recently. I was introduced to the Buddhist idea of Mindfulness. In my workshops and my coaching practice, I teach the importance of our thoughts in achieving our goals and the time had arrived to understand this lesson on a deeper level for myself.

How did I know that I was ready for the lesson?

Because firstly I came across an entire book on Mindfulness: '**The Miracle of Mindfulness**', by Thich Nhat Hanh. Just in case I hadn't got the message however another book that I was reading: '**Daring To Trust**', by David Richo, devoted an entire section to Mindfulness. Finally to really hammer home the point that this concept was important to my development, a friend was having a conversation with me and - guess what – she brought up the subject of Mindfulness also.

The Art of Mindfulness is (in a nutshell) the art of being fully present in the moment, of slowing life down and really noticing what is really happening around you. Not an easy thing to do with our hectic pace of modern life!

What has this got to do with Chickens?

Well, having a grasp intellectually of what Mindfulness consists of, is one thing, but what about in real life?

Well here my lesson was a little harsher.

I was hanging out the washing – in a rush, as I was going to meet a friend at the station. Two of my hens were enjoying themselves in the sunshine and Mabel my favourite hen rushed over to me as she always does to say hello. Rushing to put the washing out I barely noticed her by my feet.

Coming back from the station a fox shot out of our driveway and my heart sank. Coming into the garden I was greeted by a pile of feathers. The fox had got two of my hens, including Mabel. I knew there was always a risk that if you let hens roam freely that they will be taken by foxes, but I know also that the pleasure they got from being able to explore the world far out-ways the risks. But what the Art of Mindfulness had failed to teach me until that moment was that being present in the moment means enjoying what you have now – not looking forward to what is to come so much that you miss out on the present and not looking back at the past so intently that you also miss what you have now.

How many of us take our families, our friends and pets for granted?

It took the death of my hen, Ashley, to help me realise that (the story does have a happier ending, as Mabel appeared a little later minus her tail feathers but still in one piece!).

The Art of Mindfulness was one of the lessons put on my path to help me grow. Had I chosen to ignore the lesson I would have had the opportunity to learn it at another time. People often comment to me how they often choose the same types of people in a relationship (those who have a fear of commitment or who are unfaithful etc.) I tell them that spotting this common theme in their relationships is the first step to understanding the lesson their partner is trying to teach them. Once they have understood their issues surrounding the problem, they have learnt that lesson and are ready to move on and experience another area of growth. If they don't grasp the lesson, the universe will come up with more inventive ways and often more drastic ways of getting the lesson across so you cannot fail to see it!

So instead of putting your energies into survival in the modern world, why not commit them to developing into the best person you can be. Go on – I dare you to face up to those lessons that the universe is sending for you and become the hero that you are destined to be.

Use Your Mind

'They call it lost in thought because it is unchartered territory'
Quote – Anon

How often do you allow yourself time to think? Really think?

About life, your goals, your vision for the future, your hopes, your likes and dislikes?

Just stop for one second and ask yourself this question. The answer is, in many cases, not as often as you would like. Of course we have thoughts crowding our brain all of our waking hours. Shockingly however, it is believed that 95% of all the thoughts that we have each day are the same as those we had the day before. In this way we can liken our minds to ploughing the same furrow, day in day out; the furrow becoming deeper and more entrenched; consequently we struggle to think about problems differently or to come up with new ideas as we get stuck, so to speak, in this furrow.

Just imagine if you took one of your thoughts, say a long held belief and challenged it with another viewpoint.

What would it feel like? Scary? Joyful?

Sometimes when I challenge people on a thought that they are holding on to, they become angry and defensive. They want to keep hold of that thought at all costs, perhaps because they have invested too heavily in that thought to let it go (for example in terms of time and money), or they don't want to take responsibility for themselves.

For some, wasted opportunities are too painful to examine, feeling perhaps they are now too old, or stupid to pursue them now, so they continue to convince themselves that the barriers to a different choice are instead, insurmountable. But the mind continues to develop and form new pathways until the day that you die. Especially if you feed it with new experiences and ideas. Age and experience can often give you greater opportunities than would have been possible earlier in your life. But, you have to commit to using your mind to its fullest and that means allowing it to bring in original thoughts and to listening to it when it nudges you to try something different and to actively seek to challenge it when old beliefs rear up each day!

Do your old beliefs keep you from living a happy, fulfilled life?

Top 10 Tips for Tackling that Project

1. Get Excited About It

To have a clear idea about why you want to complete the project and the benefits it will bring, it will help you to get the enthusiasm you need for starting.

2. Write It Down

The act of writing down what you hope to achieve gives the project a momentum to get it off the ground.

3. Take Baby Steps

Starting a project can be daunting if you just look from where you are standing now to the finished result. But that end result is usually reached not by one monumental leap, but by lots of little baby steps along the way. Often a big project can begin with one telephone call, or, if that is too daunting by looking up the phone number. Break each action up into pieces that feel right for you.

4. Get a Support Team Together

Who do you know who will encourage you to keep going or who has knowledge that you would find useful in your project?

Do you need help with finances? Specialist knowledge?

Or just a great friend or coach who will keep you focused when you need support?

5. Make a Plan

Now you have taken the first few steps, start to make a proper plan of what will need to be done and when. Putting your ideas down on paper will stop them cluttering up your mind and becoming overwhelming.

6. What To Do When Procrastination Strikes!

If you are reluctant to take that next step in the project ask yourself:

'Why am I feeling this way?'

Is it fear (if so this is where your support team come in handy!)?

Talk it through with someone else.

Is it instinct?

Your instinct may be letting you know that it is better to wait before tackling a certain job.

Even if you are reluctant to move ahead with one part of the project, try to find other parts that you can keep moving forward with so the project doesn't come to a standstill. Keep the momentum up – eventually it will take on a life of its own.

7. Become Aware of Synchronicities / Coincidences

Do you keep meeting people who have done the same thing or can help you? Have you recently read an article on a subject that will be useful to your project?

The universe is conspiring to help you out, so keep your eyes and ears open! Equally, if you keep finding obstacles placed in your path, the timing of the project may not yet be right.

8. Shut Your Eyes and Jump Out of That Plane!

Trust that the project will now take off after all that planning.

9. When The Going Gets Tough!

There is often one part of the project in which you begin to regret starting it and you can't yet see the end of it. Hopefully the project has already taken on a momentum of its own at this point. This is the time to look back to the first steps and remember why you took it on in the first place.

Then look forward – how are you going to celebrate when you have completed the project?

Start making plans for that celebration now.

10. Celebrate!

When the project is completed, stop for a moment and acknowledge yourself.

What skills did you learn?

How good do you feel?

In stopping to celebrate how well you did, it means that when you want to tackle another project you will remember how good it felt to complete this project and how proud you were of yourself. Remember success breeds success.

A Sports Car, a Toyboy and the Kids!

What images does this title conjure up for you?

Could it be a snapshot of what we typically joke about as: 'a mid-life crisis'?

It used to be men who fell into this category, as they tried desperately to hold onto their youth. Now it seems women are joining in. However the picture does not seem as rosy as the title suggests. A survey released by the National Health Service in the United Kingdom showed that it was middle-aged women (between 35-55); in particular, who were likely to suffer from depression because they felt overloaded and stressed. On the other hand, according to the mental health charity Mind, typical symptoms of a mid-life crisis are boredom; a feeling of worthlessness; lack of meaning; and the sense that time is running out.

Well that was the bad news! The good news is that this need not be the case. For women especially (as they are often very good at adapting to the circumstances they find themselves in), mid-life can be viewed in a positive light.

In mid-life we find ourselves facing endings – not all of which are the 'happy ever after' ones we were brought up to believe in. A parent dies or depends upon us for more support, children leave home, a marriage breaks down, a career path stagnates. In the midst of all these endings however, if we chose to search for them, are the new beginnings.

Now is the time when all that you have experienced in life can be taken and moulded into a whole new life, one which the younger 'you' may never have imagined or had the bravery to go for. For now we have a sense of time running out or at least being finite, we can stop worrying about what our friends, families or the neighbours think when we suddenly become obsessed with learning to paint (or in my mother's case, belly dance).

Less obsession with our appearance and our status in the world can become more interest in what lies under the skin.

Is this shift in perspective hard to achieve?

For some yes, especially for those who have spent many years putting their own dreams on the back burner in order to raise a family, support a husband or please the parents. It can involve hard work and a widening of your comfort zone. It requires re-training your thoughts to let go of old beliefs and adopt new ones.

Think of looking out of your house onto an overgrown garden. At first you cannot see any new shoots of growth – your attention is caught by the weeds that have taken over the plot. Gradually though as you start to pull out the weeds, you find evidence of new growth underneath, different species of flowers you never imagined were there. If you are willing to commit to finding your new beginnings, who knows, the sports car, the toyboy and the kids could be a pretty good snapshot of your life!

Happy Valentine's Day

Hey You! – Yes You, I *am* talking to you! ......Happy Valentine's Day.

Let me ask you a question – today where is your attention turned?

Are you eagerly rushing to collect your post, hoping to find a card from a secret (or not so secret) admirer?

Anticipating the moment when a big bunch of flowers arrives on your doorstep?

If they have already arrived and you are already in the midst of masses of fragrant blooms, good for you. I am really happy for you. But...

For many, in fact I would go so far as to say for most people, whether single or in a relationship, they are looking for love in the wrong places. No wonder people get frustrated when they go out with person after person looking for this thing called love. Because the truth is they are making the mistake of looking in the wrong places (believe me, it took me a while to get to the truth of this one!).

Love however, is not to be found outside of yourself – love is found WITHIN you; anyone who loves you only reflects the love that you find within yourself. They do not supply it – you do!

Let me put this another way. Everybody, no exceptions, has the capacity to love himself or herself. We all started out in life loving ourselves unconditionally. Sure as we grew up circumstances/ parents/ teachers/ situations may have knocked our beliefs in our lovability; but it is still there within us. All you have to do is to look inside yourself and find it once more.

How?

You may ask. Well if you find it difficult, start small – just pause a minute and smile at yourself as you walk by a mirror – notice the twinkle in your eye / how your face lights up and appreciate yourself. Then take it a step further, when you do something you are proud of, stop and acknowledge what a wonderful person you are. Be your greatest fan. Start to notice others reactions to you. As you begin to love yourself more and more so will they, because they begin to reflect the love that you feel for yourself.

And what better day to start getting into your own 'love stream' than today?

As humans we have an enormous capacity for love; the more you feel it, the more you are able to give. Every year at this time my kids and I and any friends who happen to be around, have a big meal. I look around the table every year and think how lucky I am to have the opportunity to love so many people.

So forget the commercial Valentine's Day celebrations. Instead make it a day in which you love yourself first and then let that love spill over to your family, friends, neighbours and this year I shall include you, too.

So, HAPPY VALENTINE'S DAY!

Build Your Own Power Base

'This is the quest. To find our own power, keep it and grow it; through your career, raising a family or role in your community.'

Christine Comaford-Lynch (*'Rules for Renegades'* (2007) published by McGraw-Hill Companies).

To live an authentic life that truly makes you happy, we must often take brave decisions to quit the path we are on, or to take a U-turn where necessary. In order to do this successfully we need to build our own power base. But none of us came with instructions attached, so it is a little like trying to put together a shed when you have all the pieces but no diagram.

So where do we start?

Well let's get back to basics!

1. Get to know yourself

Spend some time putting down on paper who you see yourself as and what qualities you have.

(Write positive statements only, this is no time for negative self talk!)

Make a note of your best features.

Do not ask your friends and family for their opinion; these must be qualities that you recognise in yourself so you are not dependent upon other's opinions.

Push yourself – if you have a list of 5, aim to get to 10.

Once you have your list (for example honest, kind, compassionate, organised, beautiful eyes...) write up this list again and really stop at each quality/ feature and ask yourself why you have written that particular word (think of situations in which you have displayed that quality). Put the list to one side.

2. Write another list!

This time note down all the things you are proud of achieving in life (e.g. I was promoted twice in one year when I worked at.../ I visited my Grandmother in hospital every week before she died / I conquered my fear of flying).

When you have a list of 20+ achievements, go down the list and at each achievement note down the positive qualities you demonstrated in those situations. Add any newfound qualities to the previous list.

Now you have got a list of your qualities and achievements. Look at the two lists again.

If someone had given you these lists and told you that they described a friend of theirs, would you be impressed?

Hopefully the answer is, '*Yes*'!

If not, go back and do the two exercises again, thinking about your qualities and achievements. Be careful here that you do not underestimate your achievements. Something which may be easy for you may be difficult for somebody else. In my case, I did not think what I now consider to be my major achievement was anything special at all. I dismissed the fact that I bought up 4 children single-handedly until people kept pointing out that my children were some of the loveliest children they knew and my kids themselves look back on their childhoods as being really happy, secure and full of opportunities to develop, despite the fact we had very little money.

Now of course I realise that not only did I raise my children to the best of my ability, but also I developed other talents on the way, such as money management, leadership skills and empathy. The truth is, though, that we tend to ignore our achievements and concentrate on our failures and our weaknesses. This weakens our power base and prevents us from building an effective one. Instead we look to gain power from other sources: be it partners, job titles or money. But in truth those things are not ours to own. If we want true power, we must tap into our own source. We must be our own champions so that when we try something that doesn't work out, we will be able to get back on our feet, dust ourselves off and try again on our journey through life.

3. Make friends with yourself

Take time to really get to know how you are and what makes you happy. Look back to your childhood or times when you were happiest.

What were you doing?

Meditate and let your subconscious feed you the wisdom you possess about which direction to take.

Find a hobby which absorbs you and lets you switch off from daily life for a while, because, when you stop running around trying to please others and you start taking care of yourself, your life will become far more meaningful to you. You will get used to taking decisions based on your happiness and what you wish to achieve.

To know yourself and what makes you happy and then act upon it – that is real power.

A Celebration of Thanks

Every year in August I have a little, *'Thank You'*, ritual in my back yard. I light a fire and into it I throw pieces of paper on which I have written all the things that I am grateful for in the preceding year. Typically written on these pieces of paper are thank yous for my family; my pets; opportunities that came to me; people in my life; the work that I enjoy; and the finances which I spent on a holiday and decorating the house. Nothing earth shattering there then!

Except that I first started this ritual 15 years ago. And 15 years ago my thanks were of a very different kind. That first year that my kids and I stood over the fire throwing in our pieces of paper, I was filled with gratitude for the fact that I had found the courage to walk out of a marriage which had run its course; and that the person who had the house before us grew vegetables, so we had enough to eat in the first couple of months of being here. The kindness of strangers amazed me (my lovely next door neighbour gave me bunk-beds for the boys and a dining table). In short I was grateful for the fact that I had survived for a year on my own.

And so it is that every year I look back with wonder at how much my standard of living has improved steadily each year. I try hard to remember the feeling of gratitude I had in those early years because I don't want to forget that I have so much to be grateful for. My happiness does not increase at the same rate as my standard of living does (it is no longer the pure joy of having survived) but neither does it decrease if my standard of living goes down a peg or two.

It is a choice. We can focus our attention on what we have and give thanks for that or we can focus on what we haven't got and curse our bad luck. That is not to say we cannot strive for more, but that as we strive to improve ourselves, or our situation, we have the choice to attempt it from the perspective of gratitude for acknowledging that we already have so much that is good in our lives, that we would like to build upon these foundations.

To find this *'Attitude of Gratitude'* is one of the first key attributes in building a better life for yourself. May you always be able to count your blessings!

This is NOT The End

This is not the end.

My journey will continue.

More lessons will be learnt.

More challenges will be conquered.

I thank you for reading this far.

For information contact:

coachingtoconfidence@gmail.com

Also by Elizabeth Hill:

25 Steps to Achieving your *MAJOR* Goals – Dare to Dream

Use this page for your notes on creating your *Ideal Life*

Use this page for your notes on creating your *Ideal Life*

Use this page for your notes on creating your *Ideal Life*

37393545R00059

Printed in Great Britain
by Amazon